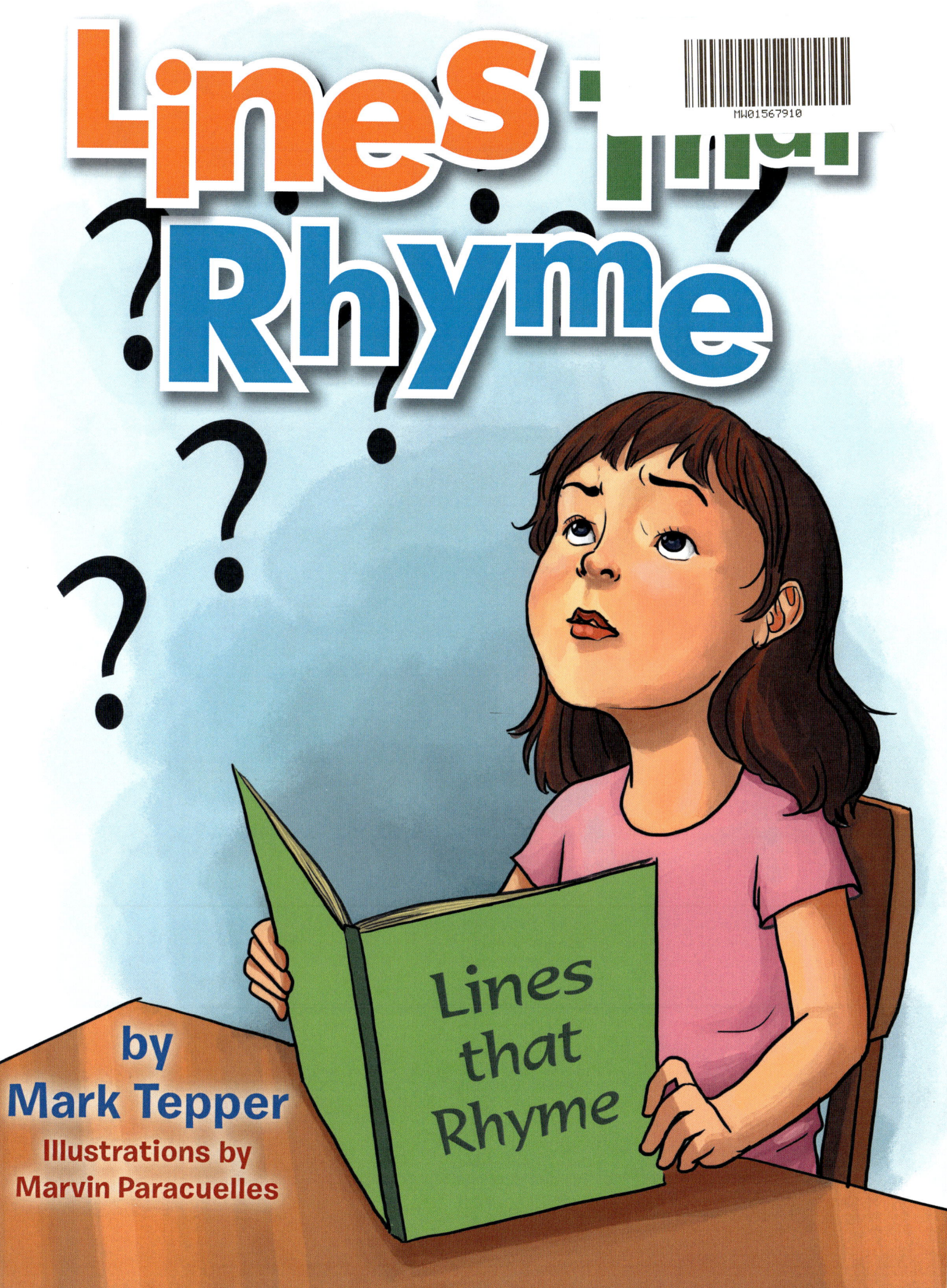

I dedicate this book to my daughter Lara, who took the time to read my riddles, and through her creative thinking brought meaning to Lines That Rhyme.

FLAT TOP

I HAVE FOUR LEGS, BUT I DON'T WALK,
YOU SIT AROUND ME TO EAT AND TALK.
SOMETIMES I'M DRESSED UP FOR THE HOLIDAYS,
OR JUST A FEW PLACEMATS FOR A CASUAL DAY.
I'M NOT A TREE, BUT I COME WITH A LEAF,
THAT WILL MAKE ME BIGGER IF YOU ADD THIS ONE PIECE.
I COULD BE BIG OR SMALL,
I COULD SIT IN A KITCHEN OR STAND IN A HALL.
I'M USED FOR HOMEWORK AND FOR GAMES,
TO MAKE BUILDING SHIPS OR MOVABLE CRANES.
I WAIT AT NIGHT FOR THE SUN'S WARM RAY'S,
MY TOP WILL BE USED THROUGHOUT THE NEW DAY.
WHO AM I?

THE ANSWER YOU SEEK IS ON THE BACK OF THE SHEET

IT ALL MAKES SCENTS

I'M A TYPE OF FLOWER, BUT NOT USED IN BREAD,
SOME OF MY COLORS ARE YELLOW, PINK AND RED.
I GROW ON A BUSH, MY STEMS HAVE LONG THORNS
THAT KEEP AWAY ANIMALS THAT MIGHT CAUSE ME HARM.
I'M USED IN BATH WATER, AND EVEN PERFUME.
MY SCENT YOU WILL NOTICE, WHEN ENTERING A ROOM.
I'M CUT AND TRIMMED AND WRAPPED IN SPECIAL WAYS,
AND GIVEN TO SWEETHEARTS ON VALENTINES DAY.
WHO AM I?

THE ANSWER YOU SEEK IS ON THE BACK OF THE SHEET

CONDUCT YOURSELF

I CAN RIDE ON TOP OR UNDERGROUND,
MY WHEELS MAKE A CLACKING SOUND.
I'M ELECTRICAL AND ALWAYS ON TRACK,
WHEN I STARTED RUNNING, I HAD A SMOKE STACK.
ALL MY CARS ARE CONNECTED TOGETHER,
AND PULLED BY AN ENGINE IN ALL TYPES OF WEATHER.
YOU'LL NEED A TICKET TO RIDE ME AROUND,
I STOP AT ALMOST ANY BIG OR SMALL TOWN.
IF YOU MISS ME, DON'T START TO WHINE,
CHECK THE SCHEDULE FOR MY NEXT ARRIVAL TIME.
WHO AM I?

THE ANSWER YOU SEEK IS ON THE BACK OF THE SHEET

POINTS OF LIGHT

LITTLE POINTS OF LIGHT THAT TWINKLE AT NIGHT,
YOU CAN'T SEE ME IN DAYLIGHT BECAUSE THE SUN IS SO BRIGHT.
I'M USED BY SAILORS TO KEEP THEIR COURSE TRUE,
WHILE SAILING ACROSS THE BIG OCEANS OF BLUE.
CONSTELLATIONS OF ANIMALS AND PEOPLE YOU'LL SEE
ALL THESE THINGS WERE MADE FROM ME.
BRING A MAP OF THE SKY TO FIND ME AT NIGHT,
I CHANGE WITH THE SEASONS, DIFFERENT PATTERNS IN SIGHT.
MY COLORS RANGE FROM PALE RED TO BRIGHT WHITE,
A TELESCOPE IS USED TO MAKE MY POINTS BRIGHT.
A WHO AM I?

THE ANSWER YOU SEEK IS ON THE BACK OF THE SHEET

SWEET TREAT

IT'S COLD AND SWEET, AND TASTES GOOD TO EAT.
IN THE SUMMER HEAT, IT'S A REFRESHING TREAT.
IT COMES WITH ALL KINDS OF TOPPINGS IN A CONE OR A CUP,
LIKE SPRINKLES, HOT FUDGE, OR WET OR DRY NUTS.
IT'S A SUNDAE, BUT YOU CAN EAT IT MONDAY
OR ANY DAY OF THE WEEK.
WHEN YOU'RE AT THE PARK OR BEACH,
IT'S AN AFTER DINNER TREAT.
THIS FROZEN TREAT WILL MELT IN HEAT,
A CUP WILL LEAVE YOU MORE TO EAT.
WHO AM I?

THE ANSWER THAT YOU SEEK IS ON THE BACK OF THE SHEET

BUZZ OFF

MY HOME IS A HIVE IN A TREE ABOVE GROUND,
I FLY ALL AROUND AND MAKE A LOUD BUZZING SOUND.
MOTHER NATURE DEPENDS ON ME,
TO DELIVER THE POLLEN TO THE FLOWERS AND TREES.
THE POLLEN IS STICKY AND SMELLS VERY SWEET,
AS I LAND ON THE PETALS, IT STICKS TO MY FEET.
I CARRY THE POLLEN FROM FLOWER TO FLOWER,
NEXT SEASON THERE'LL BLOOM WITH SOME SUN AND RAIN SHOWERS.
HONEY IS MADE IN MY HIVE THAT IS SWEET,
THEN PUT ONTO FOODS FOR THAT SPECIAL FOOD TREAT.
DON'T GET TOO CLOSE, DON'T STOP TO LINGER,
IF YOU LOOK REALLY CLOSE, I HAVE A BIG STINGER.
WHO AM I?

THE ANSWER YOU SEEK IS ON THE BACK OF THE SHEET

WET AND SOMETIMES WILD

TODAY I'M A SOLID, TOMORROW A LIQUID OR MAYBE A GAS.
YOU CAN SEE MY THREE STAGES IN YOUR SCHOOL'S SCIENCE
LAB CLASS.
AS A SOLID I COULD BE AS BIG AS A HOUSE OR FLOAT IN YOUR TEA,
I LIVE AT THE NORTH POLE OR SOMETIMES AT SEA.
THEY PUT ME IN TRAYS IN A REFRIGERATOR,
THEN INTO GLASSES WITH REFRESHMENTS FOR LATER.
AS A LIQUID, I CAN PUT OUT A FIRE OR FILL UP A POT,
YOU DRINK ME DOWN QUICKLY WHEN YOU ARE HOT.
YOU CAN SWIM IN ME OR FLOAT,
OR EVEN GO FISHING IN YOUR NEW BOAT.
WHEN TURNED INTO STEAM I CAN MOVE TRAINS ABOUT,
OR USED IN AN IRON TO GET WRINKLES OUT.
I WAS AROUND WHEN THE WORLD WAS NEW,
USE ME, DON'T ABUSE ME AND I'M ALWAYS HERE FOR YOU.
WHO AM I?

THE ANSWER YOU SEEK IS ON THE BACK OF THE SHEET

GOOD TO EAT

I CAN BE CHUNCKY OR SMOOTH GROUND,
SCOOP ME OUT AND SPREAD ME AROUND.
I'M LIKED BY YOUR BELLY,
WHEN I'M PUT ON BREAD WITH ALL KINDS OF JELLY.
I'M IN ALL KINDS OF FOOD LIKE COOKIES AND PIE,
OR PUT IN A PAN WITH BANANAS AND FRIED.
WHEN I'M NOT GROUND, AND MY SHELL TAKEN AWAY,
I MAKE A GOOD TREAT AT WORK OR AT PLAY.
I DISAPPEAR QUICKLY SO NONE WILL REMAIN.
SALTED OR PLAIN, I'M STILL THE SAME,
I'M A SNACK AT A MOVIE, A PARTY, OR BASEBALL GAME.
WHO AM I?

THE ANSWER YOU SEEK IS ON THE BACK OF THE SHEET

A TAIL THAT'S STABLE

I HAVE FOUR LEGS AND LIKE TO RUN,
BETTING ON ME COULD BE FUN.
A TRACK OF DIRT I GO AROUND,
HEAR MY HOOF BEATS ON THE GROUND.
COWBOYS USE ME TO MOVE CATTLE AROUND,
FROM OUT ON THE RANGE TO CITIES AND TOWNS.
I COULD PULL A WAGON OF HAY,
OR A SLED FOR TWO ON A SNOWY DAY.
DRESS LIKE A COWBOY AND RIDE ME AROUND,
MAKE BELIEVE YOU'RE BACK IN AN OLD WESTERN TOWN.
KEEP YOUR SECRETS, BECAUSE I TELL TALES.
I'M FOUND IN STORY BOOKS, MOVIES, AND VARIOUS FABLES.
WHO AM I?

THE ANSWER YOU SEEK IS ON THE BACK OF THE SHEET

LISTEN UP

I CAN SIT IN A CRADLE, A HANDBAG OR POCKET
OR ENCASED IN A PLACE,
ON THE BELT AT YOUR WAIST.
I'LL TALK TO ANYONE WHO WILL ANSWER ME,
I DO HAVE SOME HANG UPS
AND I'M SOMETIMES BUSY.
I'M NOT HARD TO HOLD ON TO,
BUT I'D RATHER BE HANDS FREE.
SOMETIMES I LIKE TO ROAM,
WHEN I'M FAR AWAY FROM HOME.
WITH MY ELECTRONIC RINGERS,
I CAN SOUND LIKE MOST SINGERS.
I NEED A CHARGE TO KEEP ME HIGH,
WHICH WILL KEEP ME CONNECTED TO THE NET AND WI-FI.
WHO AM I?
THE ANSWER YOU SEEK IS ON THE BACK OF THE SHEET

ALL WET

I COME IN ALL SIZES AND COLORS,
AND I'M LIGHT AS A FEATHER.
THERE'S NOTHING BETTER
WHEN WE'RE HAVING BAD WEATHER.
WITH A PUSH OF A BUTTON,
I OPEN UP WIDE,
YOU STAND UNDERNEATH ME,
FROM THE RAIN YOU WILL HIDE.
THE WIND SOMETIMES GRABS ME,
AND TURNS ME ABOUT,
I WIND UP BROKEN AND THEN GET THROWN OUT.
I'M USED AT THE BEACH TO BLOCK OUT THE SUN,
THEN REST UNDERNEATH ME WHEN YOU'RE DONE HAVING FUN.
WHEN YOU OPEN ME I'M A BIG DELIGHT,
TO KEEP YOU DRY ON A RAINY DAY OR NIGHT.
WHO AM I?

THE ANSWER YOU SEEK IS ON THE BACK OF THE SHEET

A PLACE IN SPACE

I'M BIG AND ROUND AND TRAVEL AROUND THE SUN,
I'M JUST THE RIGHT DISTANCE SO I DON'T GET BURNED.
70% OF ME IS WATER, 30% IS LAND,
I HAVE BIG DESERTS, MOUNTAINS AND A CANYON THAT'S GRAND.
THE AIR THAT SURROUNDS ME YOU BREATHE TO SURVIVE.
I ALSO GROW FOOD TO KEEP YOU ALIVE.
I SPIN AROUND AND AROUND,
WHICH HELPS KEEP YOUR FEET ON TOP OF THE GROUND.
WITHOUT THIS GRAVITY THAT HOLDS US ALL DOWN,
YOUR NEXT STOP WOULD BE SPACE WHERE YOU'LL FLOAT AROUND.
I'M EASY TO FIND WHEN YOU'RE IN OUTER SPACE,
EVERY 365 DAYS I'M IN THE SAME PLACE.
WHO AM I?

THE ANSWER YOU SEEK IS ON THE BACK OF THE SHEET

CLEAR VIEW

SOMETIMES I'M TINTED, SOMETIMES I'M PLAIN,
I LET IN SUNSHINE AND KEEP OUT THE RAIN.
A CRANK OPENS ME WIDE IF YOU TURN IT AROUND,
OR PUSH ME OPEN OR CLOSE ME TIGHT DOWN.
IF I'M TOO BRIGHT, YOU CAN COVER THE LIGHT,
WITH A CURTAIN OR SHADE THAT MOVES LEFT TO RIGHT.
YOU CAN PLACE A SCREEN IN FRONT OF ME,
TO KEEP OUT FLIES, GNATS, OR BUMBLEBEES.
KEEP ME CLEAN AND SPARKLING BRIGHT,
TO WATCH THE SUN RISE OR THE STARS AT NIGHT.
EVEN THOUGH I'M FRAMED,
I COULD BE A REAL PANE.
WHO AM I?

THE ANSWER YOU SEEK IS ON THE BACK OF THE SHEET

CENTER OF ATTRACTION

I'M PART OF YOUR FACE,
SORT OF IN THE MIDDLE PLACE.
THROUGH MY OPENINGS AIR TAKES THE BEST ROUTE;
GOOD AIR COMES IN AND BAD AIR GOES OUT.
I CAN SUPPORT THOSE FRAMES OF BLUE,
TO HELP YOUR EYES GET BETTER VIEWS.
SMELLS FROM WEAK TO STRONG,
PASS THROUGH ME ALL DAY LONG.
SOMETIMES I'M BIG OR COULD BE SMALL,
COULD BE ANY SHAPE AT ALL.
WHEN I'M RUBBED A LOT
I MIGHT GET STUFFY,
AND THEN A LITTLE RED AND PUFFY.
I'M SOMETIMES IN THE WAY,
BUT YOU KEEP ME ANYWAY.
WHO AM I?

THE ANSWER YOU SEEK IS ON THE BACK OF THE SHEET

A WAY AROUND

SOMETIMES I GO FAST OR I CAN GO SLOW,
I TAKE YOU WHERE YOU WANT TO GO.
MY COLOR, SIZE AND SHAPE GIVES ME APPEAL,
BUT UNDERNEATH I'M HARD AS STEEL.
I HAVE AN ENGINE THAT USES GAS,
STEP ON MY PEDAL TO SPEED UP AND PASS.
STEP ON MY BRAKE TO STOP OR SLOW DOWN,
WHILE OBSERVING THE SPEED LIMIT ON SIGNS IN THE TOWNS.
MY RUBBER TIRES THAT ROLL AROUND
HELP ME MOVE ALONG THE GROUND.
IF YOU MOVE IN THE WRONG DIRECTION,
YOU CAN TURN MY WHEEL TO MAKE THE CORRECTION.
THERE ARE MANY HIGHWAYS AND PLACES TO SEE,
RIDING AROUND THE COUNTRY IN ME.
WHO AM I?

THE ANSWER THAT YOU SEEK IS ON THE BACK OF THE SHEET

A FINE FEATHERED FELLOW

I BUILD MY NEST HIGH IN A TREE,
AND USE THE LEAVES AS A CANOPY.
COLORED FEATHERS OF BROWN, BLUE OR RED,
I CAN WEAR AS A VEST OR DISPLAY ON MY HEAD.
I LIKE WORMS AND BUGS THAT TASTE ALRIGHT,
BUT CATERPILLARS ARE A BIG DELIGHT.
I CAN SIT ANYWHERE BUT I LIKE TO GO HIGHER,
THE VIEW IS MUCH BETTER ON TOP OF A WIRE.
IN THE WINTER WHEN THERE'S SNOW ON THE HOUSE,
MY FRIENDS AND I WILL ALWAYS FLY SOUTH.
WHO AM I?

THE ANSWER YOU SEEK IS ON THE BACK OF THE SHEET

BLAST OFF

I STAND ON MY LAUNCH PAD
ON MY OWN SPECIAL PLACE,
READY TO FLY INTO DEEP OUTER SPACE.
ENGINES THAT MOVE ME FAR OFF THE GROUND,
SEND ME THROUGH THE AIR WITH A BIG THUNDEROUS SOUND.
AROUND THE EARTH, ORBITS TO MAKE,
WHERE ASTRONAUTS COLLECT SAMPLES
AND PICTURES THEY TAKE.
I'VE SENT PROBES TO OTHER PLANETS, IN SEARCH FOR LIFE,
TO LET THEM KNOW, THAT VISITING EARTH WOULD BE NICE.
JOHN GLENN USED ME FOR HIS FIRST TRIP INTO SPACE,
THE SPACE MUSEUM IS MY NEW RESTING PLACE.
TO VIEW CREATION, IT'S LIKE NO OTHER SENSATION.
THE FINAL FRONTIER AWAITS YOUR EXPLORATION.
WHO AM I?

THE ANSWER YOU SEEK IS ON THE BACK OF THE SHEET

CONTAINMENT

IN PREHISTORIC TIMES, I WAS MADE OF CLAY
AND LEFT TO DRY IN THE SUN ALL DAY.
SMALL CONTAINERS MADE OF GLASS
WERE FOUND IN ROMAN TIMES OF PAST.
LIQUIDS, OF MANY FLAVORS I HOLD,
MAY TASTE BETTER WHEN THEY'RE COLD.
TWISTED SHAPES AND COLORS BOLD,
MAKES THEM EASIER FOR YOU TO HOLD.
SOMETIMES MADE OF PLASTIC OR GLASS.
DON'T THROW ME AWAY WITH THE REST OF THE TRASH.
WHEN RECYCLED, I BECOME SOMETHING NEW;
TAKE ME BACK; I'LL HAVE A NICKEL FOR YOU.
PLASTIC PRODUCTS DON'T BREAK DOWN,
WHEN THEY'RE BURIED IN THE GROUND.
WHO AM I?

THE ANSWER THAT YOU SEEK IS ON THE BACK OF THE SHEET

LIGHT WORK

I'M JUST A FLICKER IN THE DARK,
TO HELP BRIGHTEN UP THE WAY,
TO LIGHTEN UP A ROOM
WHEN LOSING THE GLOW OF DAY.
I'M MADE WITH DIFFERENT COLORS
FOR PUTTING ON DISPLAY,
EACH ONE OF ME HAS DIFFERENT SCENTS,
THAT YOU CAN CHANGE EACH DAY.
I'M MADE OF WAX; IN THE CENTER THERE'S A WICK,
THAT LIGHTS FROM THE USE OF ONE MATCH STICK.
I MELT FROM THE HEAT OF THE FLAME;
AFTER A WHILE NOTHING REMAINS.
YOU CAN STILL REMEMBER ME BY THE SCENT IN THE ROOM,
BY LIGHTING A NEW ONE, THE SMELL WILL RESUME.
WHO AM I?

THE ANSWER THAT YOU SEEK IS ON THE BACK OF THE SHEET

DROPS DOWN

DARK CLOUDS FILL THE SKY,
LIGHTNING AND THUNDER SOUNDS ARE NEARBY.
I COULD BE HEAVY OR I COULD BE LIGHT,
I FALL IN DAYLIGHT AND INTO THE NIGHT.
I FILL UP RESERVOIRS AND KEEP GRASS GREEN,
THE FLOWERS LOVE ME, ESPECIALLY IN SPRING.
STRONG STORM WINDS PUSH ME AROUND,
I MAKE BIG PUDDLES ALL OVER THE GROUND.
IF IT GETS COLD, I COME DOWN AS SNOW,
CARS GET STUCK IN ME AND MAY NEED A TOW.
SKIING ON FRESH SNOW, DOWN THE HILL YOU WILL GO,
WHEN I BECOME ICE, YOU BETTER WALK SLOW.
WHO AM I?

THE ANSWER YOU SEEK IS ON THE BACK OF THE SHEET

EASY RIDER

I MOVE FAST OR SLOW ON HARDENED GROUND,
WHEN YOU PEDAL ME AROUND.
ONCE YOU RIDE ME YOU'LL NEVER FORGET,
THIS SKILL YOU'LL REMEMBER AND NEVER REGRET.
AS YOU GROW BIGGER, CHANGES ARE A MUST;
MOVE MY HANDLE BARS, RAISE MY SEAT,
MY PARTS YOU CAN ADJUST.
UP AND DOWN THE COUNTRY SIDE,
CHANGING GEARS WILL HELP YOU RIDE.
YOU CAN RIDE ME LOCAL OR DRIVE ME FAR AWAY,
YOU'LL STILL HAVE FUN AND FEEL YOUNG,
EACH AND EVERY DAY.
WHO AM I?

THE ANSWER YOU SEEK IS ON THE BACK OF THE SHEET

THE WAY IN

I HAVE TEETH BUT DON'T BITE,
IN ORDER TO WORK I SOMETIMES NEED LIGHT,
WHEN I'M NOT NEEDED I'M KEPT OUT OF SIGHT.
I'M SOMETIMES STUFFED IN A DRAWER, A PURSE OR POCKET,
BEFORE YOU LEAVE HOME YOU ALWAYS WILL LOCK IT.
DON'T LOSE ME OR YOU'LL WALK ABOUT,
YOU WON'T GET IN BECAUSE YOU'LL BE LOCKED OUT.
WHO AM I?

THE ANSWER YOU SEEK IS ON THE BACK OF THE SHEET

Made in the USA
Middletown, DE
06 February 2025